Lifelines

by

The Poetic Muselings

Michele M. Graf, Editor
Mary W. Jensen, Theme Poem
Margaret Fieland
Anne Westlund
Lin Neiswender
Kristen Howe

InkSpotter Publishing

Lifelines

To Dr Foley and the
marvelous team here —
you ladies are an appreciated
lifeline — thank you
for all you do.
  Enjoy the book —
      Michele
      5-31-12

PUBLISHED BY INKSPOTTER PUBLISHING
163 Main Avenue, Halifax, Nova Scotia, Canada B3M 1B3
http://inkspotter.com/

Cover collage © 2011 Lin Neiswender

Printed and bound in the United States of America by CreateSpace

ISBN 978-0-9813335-5-7

Also available from InkSpotter Publishing:

The August Gale (2010)
Baby Angels (2010)
Backless, Strapless & Slit to the Throat (2009)
A Boy Named Wish (2009)
Collywobblers (2008)
The Communal Desk (2009)
Dangerous Curves (2011)
Family Lines (2009)
Holiday Writes (2007)
Paper Wings (2006)
Wait a Minute, I Have to Take Off My Bra (2011)

Acknowledgements

Our Thanks To

The Muse Online Writers Conference

Not very long ago, in a kingdom that surrounds us, Lea Schizas of Montréal, Québec, had a brilliant idea: she would create an environment to nurture writers... assemble experts and mentors to provide support, encouragement, and practical assistance...so together they'd learn, thrive, and help each other continue to grow. Her goal was to make it affordable, accessible, and useful.

Carolyn Howard-Johnson, who lives in Southern California when she's not travelling all over the world, teaching, coaching, and living the writer's life, teamed up with Lea to make it real.

Thus was born the Muse Online Writers Conference, which annually draws presenters and participants from all over the world for a *free*, full week of workshops and chats on dozens of genres, web presence and how to build it, specialty niches, publishers ready for pitches of polished projects, and much more.

Lea and Carolyn provide a lifeline for creative souls. Part of the story, and what comes next, is here:

www.themuseonlinewritersconference.com

and...

The Lifelines Poetry Project

It started with a power outage in October 2008. Lisa Gentile, creativity coach from the San Francisco area, was unable to connect to the Internet and the last live chat in her Creative Block Busters workshop in the Muse Online Writers Conference.

An international group of poets waited then shared our experiences of the week: what went well; what we struggled with but were glad we persevered; and what we wanted to do with all that creative energy generated.

During this same week, Magdalena Ball, Australian author and poet, offered a workshop designed to help us develop our own chapbooks of poetry, from concept to publication. Lisa taught us to listen to what our poems were trying to tell us, and one of the messages was to keep writing. Maggie gave us the tools, vision, and courage to take that further step.

The Poetic Muselings is the result of the synergy of these workshops with Lisa and Maggie. Several of us began meeting online, shared and polished our poems, trusted ourselves and each other as we wrote bolder, sassier, riskier pieces. Our poems and purpose kept us afloat as poets and writers...and as human beings who gave and received support when it was most needed—we became each other's Lifelines.

Once we had a package we were proud of, Michele asked Lea, Carolyn, Lisa, and Maggie if they would consider mentoring us to complete the journey. All were gracious, delighted, and honored to be included.

Dear mentors and cheerleaders, thank you all for your encouragement, sage advice, and unconditional love to us, the Poetic Muselings. We hope our efforts make you proud.

Contents

About the Poets **93**

About Our Mentors **99**

tide comes in, brings life
  children play in the foam
    each wave a new lesson
      as we test the waters

Yellow's Blessing

Mary W. Jensen

a newborn, a new year
the dappled crescent of moon or banana
the sound of ribbons flapping in the breeze
curves and ruffles on an Easter dress
dancing in a field of sunflowers
the chime of bicycle bells
children jostling to ice cream truck tunes
the smell and burst of popcorn, luring the household
a trip to the salon for pedicure, massage
buttercream melting in my mouth

On Watching a Slug Die

Anne Westlund

"Let's kill it,"

my brother said, bending over to look at the dog
shit. Slugs are just snails without shells.
I read it in a book somewhere. Don't believe it though.

"Kill what? A turd?"

I learned that slugs don't flop around like bullheads
caught on a dirt bank. At the end of their slimy
trails, they just expire. It was a small slug,

"Don't you have eyes, birdbrain? That's a slug!"

so I could have called this poem "The Tragedy
of a Slug Dying Young," but its only hubris
was in being fond of sidewalks. Kevin salted it,

"Watch this."

the shaker borrowed. I think all that salt gave it heart
failure—a low-sodium slug. It shrank and stopped
moving. This wasn't much of a sign

"Dead."

of death. My brother poked it with a stick, just to be sure.
Then he ran off to play Cowboys and Indians or SS Troops, leaving
me to kick it into the bushes. Slugs don't get funerals.

Previously published in the Centennial edition of *Crosscurrents*
(University of Puget Sound, 1988)

Sitting Shiva

Margaret Fieland

Every day that year
Lou prays for his mother
at the Shul around the corner
from his sister's place.

Every day old men
shake gray bushy beards,
murmur how Lou dresses
like a Goy, no tallis
to hang below his shirt tails,
yarmulke in his back pocket,
how he speaks English to his sister,
how he's not a proper Jew.

At year end Lou walks
out of Shul into the steamy
August morning and vows
to prove them right.

Living in the River

Margaret Fieland

Pale lemon light pinks
early night sky.
A new breeze ruffles
gray dawn river waters.

All around is water,
flowing swiftly,
rising rough waves.

Small boat flails in the water.
You, a lone woman,
rest on elbows,
head tossed back,
stare up at brightening sky.

There are three of me.

One you haul into the boat,
pound on my back
as I cough, spit
brackish river water.

We drift past the other
floating on her back
staring, oblivious, at clouds.

The third, dancing on the riverbank,
you hardly glance,
pick up oars,
row vigorously by.

Water cleaves.
Light shines through
rainbow droplets.

On shore,
Ike and Tina sing.

connections made
we wade the shallows together
the tide rises,
fills spaces and lifts us up

Scorned

Lin Neiswender

You tomato lovers, avocado whores
potato purchasers, corn connoisseurs.

You go for red grapes trapped in plastic net bags
the Granny Smiths in their cool green skins
bananas transitioning from unripe to golden
while I sit here alone, Star Fruit, a foreigner scorned
with none brave enough to savor my delights.

Sweetness on the tongue like nectar
even my name is musical—Carambola—
beauty to the eye of my star's points,
sliced on the plate, waiting for your fork.

Come, be brave, embrace me
I dare you.
Heaven awaits.

Summer at the Aquarium

Anne Westlund

When we go out
dancing,
Kari dressed like some exotic fish,
Joy a Port Jackson shark,
and me more like a sea turtle,
we hang outside the exhibit in the July heat
night crowds in.

Surrounded by predators
disguised as bikers and bankers,
different variations of the same species.
The men smoke, drink, talk,
check us out,
the deadly monkey fish,
the red tail catfish,
and crowds of Mexicans
swarming like rare golden crocodiles.

Through tunnels we descend
to the bar and dancehall,
where 1,200 species
of aquatic life dance to that bump-bump
music, way too loud.

In this underwater place
there are always sharks, eels
and women like tropical fish fluttering their fins
at anyone swimming by.

Always we end up back at the petting pool,
Jell-O shots, grape and orange
Kari hooks up with a manta ray,
Joy attracts some old crab,
a shark hangs on to me for dear life,
beer on his breath, sweating bullets in a polyester shirt.

Svanesång

Anne Westlund

Two Swans

From one end of the lake
to the other.
From one end of the world
to the other.

(your song
your promise,
my pledge
my poem)

The two of us
will ruffle feathers
just walking down the street
strutting along the shore.

Will you preen for me?
in all your glory
Black Swan.

Will I defer?
in my stark beauty
White Swan.

The Meeting

When I finally land
feet splashing in Köge Bay
let through customs
my passport stamped.

Business or pleasure?

Melting into a booth
in the back of a restaurant
Grey Goose vodka on the bar
fingers touching.

What will the night bring?

A Question

Who is the traveller now?

Autumn

For now I wait,
one eye shuttered
against the future.
I send a raven
into the world.
Thoughts perch upon my shoulder
but I hold onto memory.
Leaves fall from the great tree
the wheel creaks
the wheel groans.

I call to you
across the miles
across telephone wires
strung with crows.

(I hold you
in my soft down
and feel your warmth
in the cold wind)

The Return

In the distance
I hear

an answering call.

House of Cards

Kristen Howe

You lead me to a dark place,
sneak up, blindfold me,
Fear chills my body, my heart,
when you speak.

Secret whisper, gone too far,
Dread floods my soul,
Silence, when I say, I can't handle pressure anymore.

Torture burns, weakens resolve,
A house of cards, my façade falls,
Spirit turns blue,
numb mind awakens, when I lift the blindfold.

You, kneeling, with a box,
Candlelit shadows, promises,
Your touch warms me,
A surprise—
truth.

hummingbird whispers

Mary W. Jensen

hummingbird whispers,
fleeting caresses in time—
you love, then leave me,
until the wind brings your soul
humming around me once more.

the tide turns in one last rush
         tears down sandcastles,
               buries memories,
                     leaves salt in the wounds

Maximum Fine

Anne Westlund

You're the kind of person
Who dog-ears library books
Throws them on the floor,
Cracks the spine.

Thought I could train you
To use a bookmark

Thought I could change you

I was wrong
I was wrong

I should have noticed
Before you opened my pages
Read a few lines
Then tossed me
In a corner

Back broken.

When Darkly to My Heart

Kristen Howe

Sour love, sour thorn, when darkly to my heart,
Accusations sting like angry bees in their hive,
Their honey bitter from a venom twist to start,
My tainted blood darkened by deceit to survive.

Sharp poisonous rumors pour from your toxic tone,
Your eyes lose their gleam of truth and happiness,
Dim like dying fire with few sparks to burn alone,
Your feelings dump me in a landfill mess.

There's no ring of truth to what you do or say,
Lies and half-truths aim at my bright eyes,
It feels like death to be this way,
For all that matters shatters by lies.

This thorn in my heart bleeds for our old love to be,
What once was sweet is sour, gone now darkly.

Engulfed

Margaret Fieland

Black beaded fear
forces
itself
above my right kidney,

shakes
my
hand,

spills coffee
on
my
clean white shirt.

Black bead
squeezes
itself
into my belly.

Sour
bitter
stink
rolls in my throat,

puffs
up
like a huge balloon,

draws me
down
smaller and smaller,

until I am a
pitiful
ball,

back bared,
waiting for the knife.

Fated

Anne Westlund

In a western town,
In a darkened tent
Crystal ball on the sideboard,
She peers into my hands
(There isn't enough air in here)
And tells me only dark tidings.

I stumble into the sunlight.

Love line
Life line
Line of fate
All in pieces.

Hands tell a story.
Lips tremble
Unwilling to divulge
The weight of these minutes,
Hours, days, years.

Nails adorned by polish,
Royal Flush Blush,
Fingers ringed in silver.

All I ever get are bad cards,
I throw them on the table
With my guns and walk away.

A lone cowgirl,
a desert,
a dirt road,

One last sunset.

Chief Joseph Trail

Michele M. Graf

I.

In 1877, almost 800 Nez Perce Indians, mostly women and children,
fled to resist relocation to a reservation far from their tribal lands.
When forced to surrender 40 miles from the Canadian border, they
had outmaneuvered 2000 US soldiers for 1700 torturous miles.

...Beyond unforgiving Hell's Canyon,
through the Bitterroot Mountains...
the last tragic trail of tears

II.

I am the rock,
the tiny chip of canyon wall
she clung to
when her last step
failed

I am the rock
that matched her grip,
made her part of my
ancient ruptured world,
her momentary protector

Other clans of my kind
along the jagged way
offered handholds and ledges
—or crumbled dying,
to slow pursuing hordes

her bleeding child-fingers
clutched me
and I clutched back
with all my rock strength
and spirit-etched soul

I am only a rock,
a chip of canyon wall,
horses and long guns,
brass buttons' searing glare
shattered my spine

I am a rock,
a chip of canyon wall,
weeping

the tide retreats
      leaves hollow places, empty of life's waters
          those on the shore watch,
              long for what was taken

Princess of the Waters

Mary W. Jensen

Some call them Children of Neptune,
mermaids, sirens of the sea
we three brothers
on our small fishing vessel
bestowed a name
on she

the first time
a splash
gone missing
a pocket watch
a shoelace

next time
a flash of golden eyes
peering along water's surface
'neath twisted strands of hair

we tempted her
with baubles left on boat's edge
in return she teased us
with glimpses of ivory skin

a fortnight it took
to earn her trust
the moon a silver coin
glinting from waters

new charm in hand
she pulled herself atop a rock
dripping hair and dark seaweed
clinging to curves

nimble fingers wove bracelet
into layers of hair
next to the watch chain
and a broken
seashell
tied with shoestring

musical trills greeted us
as our boat rowed nigh
dolphins came to join her song
'twas then we named her
Sabrina
princess of the waters

a sultry smile
a curl of finger
beckoned us to join her

our youngest brother did not hesitate
to slide into dark waters
lean on the rock beside her
she cupped his face
kissed him
mouths still joined she dove
taking him into the sea

so jealous were we
at the attention
the boat swayed as
we stood to join them
but the dolphins leapt
intercepting our every move

three now two
each night we return
yearning for another glimpse
bearing gifts in hope
for the prize of her kiss

each night in vain
she needs us no more
Sabrina has chosen her prince

Previously published in *Moon Drenched Fables* (Sept 2009)

Hoof Prints in the Sand

Anne Westlund

How bittersweet
       this day
       this fine loneliness.

Crowds of people
       don't see me, don't acknowledge me.

Sounds of motors, raised voices
       underneath it all, wind blows sand
       over the beach, until it settles on everything.
Driftwood rises out of the sand
       like fallen Roman columns.
A gray haze covers all.

Tourists wear sunglasses
vainly hope for sunshine.
Waves crash beyond
the line of cars.
       Sweet smell of horseshit
       sharp scent of a fire
drift on by and disperse, like broken promises.

Tucked in next to a log,
bag from Uwajimaya on the sand,
bluer than the sky above,
pen at the ready,
nothing inspires me
on this familiar beach
a couple miles from home.

Nothing.
Nothing at all.

Just Once

Lin Neiswender

I'd like to do something unexpected,
like streak across the quadrangle
at 2 A.M. bare butt naked,
or have one too many, maybe
tell my boss what I really
think of him.

I want to taste juicy forbidden fruit,
speed along at ninety miles an hour,
fly to far-off Bali's Uluwatu beach
to soak up sunshine for a weekend.

Just once I'd like to shake off respectability
like fleas from a dog and be downright bad.

But right now I've got to finish writing
this sermon.

Some Day

Lin Neiswender

Raging, I pack away
fine china,
silk sheets,
candles too fancy for every day,
perfume from exotic lands,
that expensive sheer nightgown I was saving
for some red letter evening—
not needed now.

I can't bear them around me.

I rip coverlets off the sofa
beat pillows, where
I so often complained
about dirty shoes on the couch,
your sweaty head on the cushions.

If only they were here now,
I wouldn't save the good things
for some day.

Waiting

Michele M. Graf

Is it time?

I want to know the pain is over
your haunted spirit
calm and empty
all dragons slain

No more tortured nights
and bleaker days

Are you afraid to say goodbye?

Your life choices
all came due
you pay
with each struggled breath

Can you forgive what's in my heart?

I want to mourn,
say god speed
shalom
peace be with you

Stand by your graveside
feel the earth settle and sigh

place the traditional stone
in remembrance
and goodbye

Who am I to say accept your fate?

I am weary, spent,
gut-wrenched
watching,
waiting

Will you give us back our lives
while we still care?

life carries us
　　　　out to sea
　　　　　　childhood's shore
　　　　　　　　left on the horizon

Losing Your Way on Memory Lane

Margaret Fieland

You leave $5 you stole from the candy store
in the rest area ladies room,

throw your father kissing his secretary
out the car window,

stash your broken marriage
behind the seat,

forget you're tone deaf,
belt out blues tunes
you wished you could sing.

Too bad you won't remember
finding your voice.

The Warmth of Orange

Mary W. Jensen

harvest
subtle cinnamon and nutmeg in pumpkin pie
chocolate oranges, melting and sweet
old sepia photographs
a worn recliner
a life vest, a raft, a hug
being rocked in your mother's arms
a lullaby
a stuffed animal
snuggling under the quilt
the smell of a heater awakening for winter

Galileo Oh

Lin Neiswender

What a pain of the heart
To try and reconcile
What you know to be true
In your innermost being
With what others have decided
Is the only truth you are allowed
To have and hold, regardless
Of what your own eyes and brain
Recognize and comprehend

Oh Galileo Galilei, brave one,
They bowed your body but not your mind
That stayed free and roamed the rings of Saturn
Followed the ellipse around the sun

Even in your blindness you could see
That sunlight God sent from the centre outward
From His heart to ours, enlightened the night
One theory, one truth, one sight

An Old House in Six Degrees

Lin Neiswender

Roof on vacant house
sags, may yet break from weight
a vast pillow of snow, like Atlas dropping
to one knee, a world too heavy
for one with his silver head.

Weathered boards creak in the wind,
shutters throw a tantrum
as they clatter in the snowstorm.

Icicles glisten along the roof line
Still, cold daggers waiting to descend.

the sea takes us
        pulls us into its depths

hunger

Michele M. Graf

midnight tide
ripples with undertow
drinks me in,
binds my fears,
lines the moray eel's den
with my sticky inhibitions

all frazzle and fight
seeps and flows
into diluted distance

spirit freed
from its brittle shell
senses
brined and open
I stalk the ancient shark
offer my entrails
and intuitive mind
yield and embrace

slither in
where ocean breathes
and fishes sigh

fluid as the sea
my molecules meld
to spaces
within spaces

curiosity sated
I slide down
smooth
and
glowing

like
the moon
swallowed
whole

Mother's Day

Margaret Fieland

He died
the white-haired doctor
with smiling eyes,

leaving you
to the quick-voiced young one,
who called your cramps indigestion.

Your hair became
sparse as grass during a dry August,

your walk
creaky as the old pasture gate,

your frame as thin
and brittle as bare branches
of the old oak.

until finally
you lay in bed, smelling
of old guts, too weak
to lift your head.

We named
the baby
after you

Ode to a Dead Cigar

Margaret Fieland

Chess game unfinished,
baseball game unwatched,
daily paper unread—

Pneumonia invaded old lungs
choked from years
of cigars and pipes.

He's gone and I inhale
memory of stinging smoke
and smoke of stinging memory.

Restless Peace

Michele M. Graf

I remember...

...How excited you were
to start college at fifty-three,
wanted me to be part of it,
but how nervous I made you.

...Your camel ride,
and how you danced the Hora
without your cane
the last night in Israel.

...Your glitter days of decorating,
the treasures you collected—
herd of elephants,
music boxes, clowns,
gypsy violins,
Lladro figurines.
And flowers—
velvet red roses, especially.
Raw, returning reminder
of sorrow's bloom.

...You were loyal to your friends,
ecstatic with their triumphs,
anguished in their agony,
fiercely protective of those in need.

...You felt whole when you gave
beyond your limits
of time and energy and hope
then crashed. Again.

And I remember...

...All the times we dealt
in guilt and blame,
held onto hurts and slights,
refused to let them heal.

...Your choices tore us apart,
those left behind.
Impossible to make peace
with your unfinished business.

...You told me, even at the end,
we were supposed to keep arguing.
When you stopped fighting,
I'd know you'd given up.

...We swapped mother-daughter roles
several lifetimes earlier.
I couldn't parent you any better
than you tried to do with me.

...You had the last word
when you died. Why
do I keep arguing with you still?

the tide turns again
nature brings in new life
to replace the lost;
an endless cycle

on the beach

Michele M. Graf

wave action and tide
 bring green foam,

  crabs, translucent jellyfish,
   dead sea lions
    and baby seals

     vultures, sea gulls, crows
      —the next wave—

      recycle and rearrange
     what tides ignore

     only skull-shells,
    spinal bones
   and tail fin

  driftwood shards
 of echoed spirit
are left now

on the beach

Brush Strokes

Michele M. Graf

Winter

Belief

I envy people
so sure God will provide—
I pray they are right

Spring

Peace

soft blossoms of snow
frame the timeless untrod road
wait for springtime
yearn for one simple sound—
healing hope, and all tears shed

Summer

After Tai Chi

calm, touched to the core
all life is in this moment
breath, grateful, in place

Autumn

Forty Years of Love

Fear not love's end
or what's left of life's journey
linked hearts transcend time
our kite string holds as we fly
with dreams that still kiss clouds

Stargazing
Kristen Howe

Bright

Twinkling   Supernovas   Sparkling

Far away   Heavenly   Mythical   Constellations

Tiny   White   Shining   Orbs

Golden   Clusters

Telescopes   Glowing   Light

Awestruck   Astronomy

Streaming Stars

Mary W. Jensen

Around my shoulders, I wrap the night,
As I perch on the mountaintop;
Delight shivers through me,
Anticipates the sight.

The first light darts across the sky
Followed by more streaming stars,
So bright until they disappear.
Wishes will be born tonight.

I do not envy meteors' plight—
Lights so quickly burning out—
But in my heart they persevere
In splendid and untamed flight.

incoming waters
  bring inspiration,
    new beauties
      and life experiences to discover

Voice of Eloquent Silence

Kristen Howe

Alone in silence,
My heart is peaceful as ocean,
clean as air.
Burden lifted,
My creativity soars.

Once empty well now full.
Organized. Energized.
Peaceful mind.
Safe as a locked vault.

Raw Sienna

Lin Neiswender

How I love that name, Raw Sienna.
Elixir of cinnamon and rusty nails
Red earth mother's war paint.

Favourite of classical artists long passed
And brash colour-slashers of modern times
heats up the view wherever it's found.

Hue that reappears in fashion too,
incarnation of cycled euphemism
for grounding, grinding, earth tones.

Song of colour, in-your-face real,
hits you in the gut then
rises to a high note of power,
trails to a whimper,
so you never ever forget her melody,
Raw Sienna.

Infinity and Beyond

Kristen Howe

We penetrate clouds like birds.
Peel back skin of our planet to sunny blue sky
Gravity's pull releases our dream ship, now
A dot on intergalactic map.

Beyond sun's ultraviolet rays,
A thousand myths shine bright ahead
We resist Black Hole's pull.
One supernova electrifies night.

We soak up glows from a passing full moon,
Our journey a dream fulfilled,
And gently, retrace our path back to earth
From infinity and beyond.

Never Doubt

Kristen Howe

Never doubt your instincts or your dreams to
reach for the stars, glowing in the dark,
like captured fireflies in their
bell jar, flittering their wings
to break free and escape
with burning embers
that launch fire to
fuse your goals
make them
one

The Essence of Violet

Mary W. Jensen

twilight, anything is possible
gumballs, jellybeans, lollipops
banners flying from a castle
dragon scales and fairy tales
music that demands dancing
the scent of lilacs
picnics in the park
a muse playing hide and seek
first kiss, trembling discovery
the bee's impossible flight
half remembered dream

About the Poets

Join our Poetic Muselings journey as we share our poetic lifeline with the world.

poetic-muselings.net

Explore wacky tangents, images, ideas for our inner poets,
editing tips, poetic forms, collaborative writing techniques,
favourite finds, marketing, artistic expression,
and how we experience the world—
passionate, incongruous, and
embracing our creative,
poetic voices.

Michele M. Graf

Michele M. Graf is an eclectic writer and editor of poetry, novels, screen-plays, essays, and other nonfiction. *Heart, Soul, and Rough Edges*, a coffee table book of poetry, prose, and photos to capture the decade-long, 100,000-mile journey through the US and Canada that she and her husband lived, is coming together. She creates art on her computer and practices Tai Chi when she remembers to breathe.

Michele's been published online and in print and is Poetry Editor for the award-winning *Apollo's Lyre* E-zine (apollos-lyre.tripod.com). Gluten-Free Travel by Graf (glutenfree-travel.blogspot.com) is a resource for people with celiac disease and other forms of gluten intolerance. Her other online home is RoadWriter (roadwriter.net), and you can also find her on LinkedIn (linkedin.com /pub/michele-graf/6/6a4/a99).

Michele is Leader of the Mod Squad—the chat moderators, transcript takers, and other behind-the-scene support folks—for the annual Muse Online Writers Conference. She's active in the Willamette Writers, Oregon Poetry Association (OPA), the Lane Literary Guild, and two poetry critique groups. She now lives in Oregon with her husband of a thousand years, and an adopted Standard Poodle, the Alpha Female of the pack.

"The Poetic Muselings were my lifeline, surrounding me with love and support during an extremely stressful time. We've never met in person, but I treasure these kindred spirits and wonderfully rowdy poets. And Carolyn, my first poetry mentor—see where it led?"

Mary W. Jensen

Mary W. Jensen lives in Utah with her husband and son. She's the middle of nine children and escaped the loud-ness of reality by immersing herself in books and poetry. From chaos comes creation.

Her poetry has been published in the webzines *The Pink Chameleon*, *Moon Drenched Fables*, and *Abyss & Apex*. Mary is a moderator on Writing.com, an online writing community, and was an editor for their fantasy newsletter for two years. She has various incarnations online under the designation Feywriter, including a twitter account (twitter.com/feywriter), and keeps a blog (marywjensen.blogspot.com).

"I never would have written *Princess of the Waters* if not for the inspiration of the Muse Conference. This group gave me the support and feedback that led to my publication. Lisa, thank you for helping me to break free of form and really listen to my poems."

Margaret Fieland

Born and raised in Manhattan, Margaret Fieland has lived in the Boston area since just after the blizzard of 1978, thus missing the opportunity to abandon her car in a snow bank and walk home. She now lives outside Boston with her partner and a large pack of dogs. In spite of earning her living as a computer software engineer, she turned to one of her sons to put up the first version of her website, a clear illustration of the computer generation gap. An accomplished flute and piccolo player, she is also able to write backwards and wiggle her ears. Thanks to her father's relentless hounding, she can still recite the rules for pronoun agreement in both English and French.

Her articles, poems, and stories have appeared in anthologies and journals such as *Main Channel Voices*, *Front Range Review*, and *All Rights Reserved*. Her book *Relocated* will be available from MuseItUp Publishing in July 2012. Another book, *The Angry Little Boy*, will be published by 4RV Publishing in early 2013. Her website is margaretfieland.com.

"The revision process for this anthology was a real eye opener. Sometimes what turned out to be the key insight, for me, in a particular poem, came from what at first appeared to be a casual comment by a fellow Museling."

Anne Westlund

Anne Westlund attended the University of Puget Sound in Tacoma, where she majored in Creative Writing/English Literature and co-edited *Crosscurrents Review*, the school's literary magazine. She still lives in Western Washington, near the coast with her cat, Betty Boop.

Her poem "Fur" was published in the *Marshall Creek Newsletter*. Anne was an integral part of "Poetry Potpourri," a poetry reading by local poets held at the Aberdeen Timberland Library in the Spring of 2009. She is putting together a book of poetry based on the Viking Runes. Anne is enrolled in a Masters Program for Interfaith Studies. When not studying, she can be found crafting, cooking, playing computer mahjong, or surfing creativity websites. Anne is active in CoachCreativeSpace (coachcreativespace.ning.com). Please visit Anne at flavors.me/annepoptart for links to all her websites.

Anne's poem "My Town" and two of her photographs will be published in Ocean Seminary College's *Restoration Earth Journal* Issue 1, Volume 1, this fall.

"I didn't revise my poems much before this group. In Lisa Gentile's class at the Muse Conference, I learned how editing improves poems. We put the idea into practice in our Poetic Muselings group. This was a moment of growth for me as a writer."

Lin Neiswender

With the rich language of her Alabama surroundings firing her imagination, Lin Neiswender knew from childhood that she was destined to be a writer but lacked the courage to follow her dreams until her later years.

She now lives in Central Florida. The change in climate agrees with her, as she has finally blossomed into a bonafide writer. Her short stories and poetry have appeared in print and online. Lin spends her spare time collaging and working in mixed media, making jewellery, exploring creative sites on the Internet, and playing with her animals, a feisty female kitty with cattitude and a Shetland sheepdog who thinks it is his job to try to eat the mailman.

Reach her through her poetry blog, Lin Neiswender: The Poet in Me (linneiswenderpoetry.wordpress.com), or her personal blog, Land of Lin (landoflin.blogspot.com).

"Poetic Muselings has been a blessing to me in terms of furthering my craft and making deep friendships with the participants. I have learned so much from these people. I've grown as a person as well. Thank you, Muselings!"

Kristen Howe

Kristen Howe was born in Englewood Heights, New Jersey, and raised in Rockaway, New Jersey. She now resides in Cuyahoga Falls, Ohio, with her two cats. She's the younger of two children and loves to read books and research online.

Kristen's been previously published in a variety of ezines and magazines, including the *Pink Chameleon Online*, *Pulse*, *Long Story Short*, and *The Mid-America Poetry Review*. Kristen's currently querying her first novel, an eco-thriller, *Venom*.

She has two blogs (kristensbookjungle.blogspot.com

and kristenswritingendeavors.wordpress.com). She's also available on Twitter @Kristen_Howe.

"I would never have gotten this far without the help of my friends and mentors, to go further in my poetry, and would like to thank my fellow Muselings for the encouragement and feedback. To Michele, thanks for believing in me and my poetry."

About Our Mentors

Lea Schizas

Lea Schizas has been around the writing world for over twelve years, edited for several publishing houses, founded the annual Muse Online Writers Conference (themuseonlinewritersconference.com), and is the founder and publisher of the award-winning ezine *Apollo's Lyre* (apollos-lyre.tripod.com).

Her websites have been mentioned in Writer's Digest Top 101 Writing Sites and won several awards in various categories in the Preditors and Editors annual voting polls. Writers have referred to her as Mother Hen because of her caring nature to help and mentor writers around the world.

And now, she offers another way to help writers, with MuseItUp Publishing, a small Canadian e-press specializing in high-quality e-books.

MuseItUp Publishing (museituppublishing.com): Where your Muse entertains readers in mainstream genres, including mystery, thrillers, paranormal, fantasy, romance, horror, dark fiction, sci-fi, and young adult.

MuseItHOT! (museithotpublishing.com): Because we have what you want on our erotica romance website. Caution: ADULT CONTENT!

Magdalena Ball

Magdalena Ball was born in New York City, where she grew up. After gaining an honours degree in English Literature from the City University of New York (CCNY), she moved to Oxford to study English Literature at a postgraduate level. After a brief return to the US, she then migrated to NSW Australia, where she now resides on a rural property with her husband and three children. While in Australia she received a Masters degree in Business from Charles Sturt University and a Marketing degree from the University of Newcastle.

Magdalena runs the well respected review site The Compulsive Readers (compulsivereader.com/html/). Her short stories, editorials, poetry, reviews, and articles have appeared in a wide number of printed anthologies and journals, and she has won local and international awards for poetry and fiction. She is the author of the poetry books *Repulsion Thrust* and *Quark Soup*, the novel *Sleep Before Evening*, a nonfiction book *The Art of Assessment,* and, in collaboration with Carolyn Howard-Johnson, the Celebration Series poetry books *Deeper Into the Pond, Blooming Red, Cherished Pulse, She Wore Emerald Then,* and *Imagining the Future.* She also runs a radio show, The Compulsive Reader Talks.

In addition to her writing, Magdalena is an information and commercialisation advisor for a multi-national company, sometimes teaches writing classes in a variety of venues and on a variety of topics, does the odd bit of book editing, and, regardless of what she's doing, will usually be found with a book or two in one form or another, sneaking time for reading, her first love.

For more on Magdalena, please visit her website at magdalenaball.com.

Carolyn Howard-Johnson

Carolyn Howard-Johnson is a multi award-winning novelist and poet. Her fiction, nonfiction, and poems have appeared in national magazines, anthologies, and review journals. A chapbook of poetry, *Tracings*, was named to *The Compulsive Reader*'s Ten Best Reads list and was given the Military Writers' Society of America's Silver Award of Excellence. Her Celebration Series of chapbooks have also won multiple awards. She speaks on tolerance, writing, and book promotion and has appeared on TV and hundreds of radio stations nationwide.

She is an instructor for UCLA Extension's world-renowned Writers' Program, and the second edition of her multi award-winning how-to book, *The Frugal Book Promoter* (www.budurl.com/FrugalBkPromo), was just released to rave reviews. *The Frugal Editor: Put Your Best Book Forward to Avoid Humiliation and Ensure Success* is also an award winner, and that book won the marketing award from New Generation Book Awards. She was also named Woman of the Year in Arts and Entertainment by members of the California legislature.

Lisa Gentile

Lisa Gentile M.S. is a life coach for moxie mavericks (moxiemavericks.com)—people who are willing to get creative to make big things happen in their lives. Lisa helps her clients identify and leverage their core strengths to create maximum satisfaction and impact in their endeavors, utilizing evidence-based coaching techniques, valid, reliable, and effective approaches.

Lisa draws on her training in psychology, education, business, and coaching as well as her experience in organizational development, marketing, and strategic planning. She earned her B.A. in Experimental Psychology at Revelle College at University of California San Diego and her M.S. in Education & Psychological Studies at California State University East Bay. She received her professional coaching-specific training from Coach Training Alliance, VIA Institute, and Fielding Graduate University.

Outside of her coaching practice, Lisa maintains a life-long interest in making art. She is a crafter, a visual artist, a published poet, a National Novel Writing Month winner, a playwright, a screenwriter, and a film director. Three plays that she co-wrote with her husband, Nick, have been performed in California. Their films have premiered at the California Independent Film Festival and the Danville International Children's Film Festival. Lisa and Nick enjoy sailing and traveling from their home base in the San Francisco East Bay Area.

Made in the USA
Charleston, SC
05 February 2012